High-Frequency READERS™

W9-AWP-980

We Like Fruit

Written by Millen Lee
Illustrated by Tungwai Chau

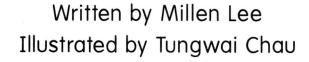

Scholastic Inc.
New York   Toronto   London   Auckland   Sydney
Mexico City   New Delhi   Hong Kong

Copyright © 2000 by Scholastic Inc.
SCHOLASTIC, HIGH-FREQUENCY READERS, and associated logos and designs are
trademarks and/or registered trademarks of Scholastic Inc.
All rights reserved. Published by Scholastic Inc.
Printed in the U.S.A.
ISBN 0-439-06462-7

4 5 6 7 8 9 10   23   05 04 03 02 01 00

We go to the store.

I like apples and oranges.

I like oranges and pears.

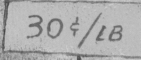

I like pears and peaches.

Peac

I like peaches and bananas.

I like bananas and strawberries.

We like fruit.